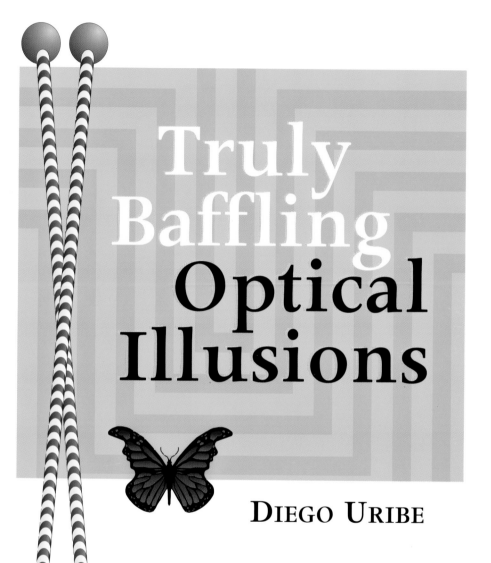

Truly
Baffling
Optical
Illusions

DIEGO URIBE

Sterling Publishing Co., Inc.
New York

Acknowledgments

I would like to express my gratitude to Mitsumasa Anno, Paul B. Arnold, Bruno Ernst, Richard Haas, Mathieu Hamaekers, Fred van Houten, Scott Kim, André Martins de Barros, Sandro Del-Prete, István Orosz, and Gianni A. Sarcone for their kind permission to use their work. I would also like to thank Robert Llywelyn, from Portmeirion, for the use of the photos of the Unicorn Cottage. And, finally, to Itsuo Sakane, Joseph W. Dauben, and Joseph Romano (Oberlin College), for their assistance in finding material for this book and obtaining permissions.

Library of Congress Cataloging-in-Publication Data

Uribe, Diego, 1955-
    Truly baffling optical illusions / Diego Uribe.
       p. cm.
    Includes index.
    ISBN 1-4027-0557-3
    1. Optical illusions. I. Title.
QP495 .U75 2003
152.14'8--dc21

                   2003008371

10 9 8 7 6 5 4 3 2 1

Published by Sterling Publishing Co., Inc.
387 Park Avenue South, New York, NY 10016
© 2003 by Diego Uribe
Distributed in Canada by Sterling Publishing
c/o Canadian Manda Group, One Atlantic Avenue, Suite 105
Toronto, Ontario, Canada M6K 3E7
Distributed in Great Britain by Chrysalis Books
64 Brewery Road, London N7 9NT, England
Distributed in Australia by Capricorn Link (Australia) Pty. Ltd.
P.O. Box 704, Windsor, NSW 2756, Australia

Manufactured in China

Sterling ISBN 1-4027-0557-3

Contents

What Are Optical Illusions?

Compare the two matchboxes above. They appear to have different dimensions: the left one is longer than the right one. Would you believe that this is an optical illusion? Copy this page, cut out the matchbox tops, and place one over the other. They will match exactly.

Some people may think that this is not an illusion. If we took two actual matchboxes of this shape, positioned them the same way, and then took a photograph of them, the image would be similar to the illustration.

But if we removed the familiarity of the items and simply made them two geometric shapes that are the same dimensions as the matchbox tops (see below), then why does the left one still appear longer than the right one?

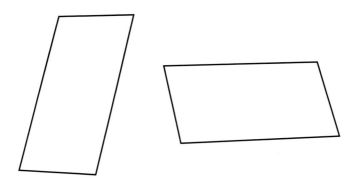

This illusion raises the types of questions scientists ask themselves: Why do our eyes occasionally fool us? Why, although we know two objects are alike, do we persist in seeing them as different? Is this because of some fault in our visual system? Research has shown that the last question is not the case.

Optical illusions show us how we perceive things. There have been different opinions on where the illusion occurs. Some theories state that the illusion originates in the eye, others state that it is in the brain, which processes and decodes the data captured by the eye. Even in the latter theory there are wide divergences of opinions on exactly how the brain decodes the information. Are we born with a "pre-programmed" brain, do we develop these decoding skills, or is this simply a reflexive response similar to the knee-jerk reaction that doctors give us when they tap our knee with a small hammer? These questions are still being explored by scientists.

Beyond the scientific aspect of optical illusions, they are great fun to view. They intrigue and entertain us. Many artists, such as Salvador Dalí or M.C. Escher to name the more popular, used optical illusions in their works. Op art, or optical art, was a movement based on visual illusions. Throughout the book, and especially in the Illusions Gallery (see page 105–117), you will find some of them.

This book is broken into short chapters dealing with different types of illusions. Except for a very few, they can be read in any order you like. If you find a reference to a chapter you haven't yet read, you may want to take a quick look at it and then return to your reading. You will need no special knowledge. A few somewhat more technical chapters are placed at the end of the book, which you may prefer to read last.

Now, the illusions!

Foreground and Background

The above illustration is composed of two elements: the figures in the foreground and the white background. At first sight, the illustration shows three rows of butterflies. The butterflies in the first row are the most lightly colored, the butterflies in the second row are darkened, and the ones in the last row are black. But if you look closer, you will see something more: the white background area around the wings shows the profiles of faces. These two figures represent complementary objects: the wings' borders (the foreground) define the faces while the faces (the background) define the wings.

Notice that the profiles stand out more along the bottom row. The greater the contrast between the foreground and background, the better both are perceived.

Now that you have some understanding of foreground and background relationships, here's the next illusion. The figure below shows a goblet. What does the background show?

Answer on page 120.

The foreground-background relationship can be used in other ways. In the illusion below, graphic artist Fred Hausmann plays with white foreground figures and dark red background figures. But, at the same time, the white figures can be seen as the background while the dark red figures are seen as the foreground. In this illusion the foreground and background can switch depending upon how you look at it.

In the next illustration by Gianni Sarcone, the foreground and background changes meaning depending upon how the scene is perceived. If you see a bear getting out of the water, the dark patch is a hole in the ice. If you see a black seal, the lines that represented the bear head and claws are now pebbles and scratches in the ice.

'96, G. Sarcone, Lausanne

Sam Loyd, a famous American puzzle creator who lived a century ago, did the following illusion. The donkey below is made of six pieces: body, four legs, and tail. Photocopy the illustration, cut out the parts, and rearrange them to create a galloping horse.

HINT: Remember, this chapter is on foreground and background.

Answer on page 120.

The Shape of the Eye

We all have round eyes (or, better, almost spherical). Hence, our retinas, the part of the eye where the image we are looking at is projected, are curved. This can be easily verified by closing an eye and bringing the illusion below up to the other eye until your nose touches the page. It will be out of focus but you can still perceive the following effect. When the book is farther away, the inner squares are smaller than the outer and the borders are curved. As the illustration comes closer, the borders begin to straighten up and all the squares tend to look alike. You can even reach the point where the board can be seen as a perfect square.

This happens because the image seen from afar is projected onto a small, flat area of the retina. When you bring the image close enough, it almost covers the complete retina so that the curvature of the eye and the curvature of the checkerboard cancel each other out.

Lettering

Practicing calligraphy is usually done on lined notebooks. One line indicates the base upon which letters should be traced. Another line marks the exact height of the lower cases. A third line is for the height of the capital letters and ascenders (e.g., b, d, f). A last line is for the descenders (e.g., g, j, p). To the layman's eye, this looks like a very precise art. Or is it?

Of the two versions of the word "exact" (shown below) which word's letters (except for the t, of course) have the same height? Most will pick the top one. In the lower one, the x looks slightly higher than the e, a, and c. However, it's the other way round: the word with all letters exactly the same height is the lower one.

exact
exact

To prove this, the following page shows an enlargement of the three first letters of the top word placed between guides. The curved parts of the letters overlap the guides. For example, the tail of the letter a rests on the guide but its front overlaps it. Curved areas of a letter, when compared with straight ones, have a tendency to look shrunk and fill less space. Hence, to compensate and make it look the same size, these areas must be enlarged. Calligraphy, as well as typography, employs these little adjustments to provide a uniform look.

exa

Here is another example of symmetry. Take a look at these two S's. The one on the left looks perfectly symmetrical while the one on the right looks lopsided. The upper part of the S looks disproportionately larger than its bottom.

Once more, this is not the case. The upper part of the left S is smaller than its lower half while the right S is symmetrical. You can see this by turning the letters upside down.

S S

Now it's the S on the left that looks lopsided while the one at the right did not change.

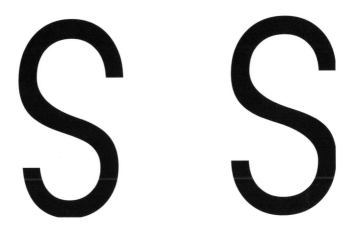

Let's put to use your newly acquired knowledge on perception to solve the following illusion. The four geometric figures below all look to be the same height. As you have probably guessed, they aren't. Can you rearrange them from tallest to shortest without measuring them?

Answer on page 121.

A Hole in the Eye

We all have holes in our eyes: one hole in each eye. And in the very place where the hole is, we are blind. You can easily check this. Place the book level at about a foot (30 cm) away from you. Close your right eye and fix your left eye on the little green square on the page. (If you prefer using your right eye, then turn the book 180° but still keep it level).

Slowly bring the book toward you. Keep your eye fixed on the green square. At a certain point, the smiling face will disappear.

To understand why the face disappeared, we must first make a brief description of the eye. Light enters the eye through the pupil, the dark part at the center of the iris. (The iris is the colored area of the eye; when we say a person has blue or brown eyes, we mean the iris.) Behind the pupil, the crystalline lens focuses and projects the light coming from images into the retina, which covers the inner back of the eye. Were we to compare the eye with a camera, the crystalline would be equivalent to the camera lens, the iris is the diaphragm (which opens when light is dim and closes when bright), the pupil is the diaphragm aperture, and the retina would be the film. The retina is made up of thousands of light sensitive cells. Each of these cells is "wired" to a nerve. When light falls on it, the cell sends a tiny electrical signal that travels along the nerve. All the nerves coming from the cells make a bundle, called the optical nerve, that carries the signals to the brain (which acts as an image processing computer). The spot where the optical nerve goes through the retina has no light sensitive cells. This is the blind spot, or the hole in our eye.

You may ask: If we have holes in our eyes, then why do we see complete scenes with no gaps in them? Because our brain constructs the image at the blind spot by considering its surroundings. You have just experienced it: when you looked at the first illustration, your brain replaced the smiling face with the paper surrounding it.

Now you can check it again with the illustration below. As you did before, close you right eye, level this book, and look directly at the little square with your left eye. Remember to fix your sight. Slowly bring the book closer. When the smiling face coincides with your blind spot, your brain will fill the hole by completing the surrounding rays.

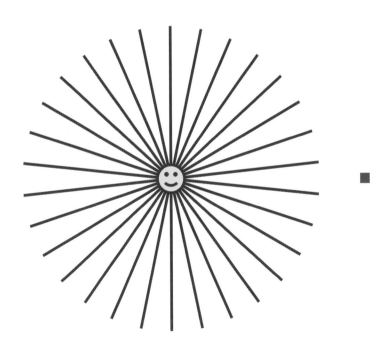

The brain fills the blind spot in intriguing ways. Unlike the previous illusion, this illusion does not complete the central horizontal line. Instead, you will see a white vertical column.

However, if the lines are sparser (and, hence, the white column is not well defined), then the brain completes the line that the face is resting on.

Now you can do your own experiments. Try using two lines, where one is longer than the other or a different color, that cross at your blind spot. You can also try a circle that is divided into halves painted in different colors with the smiling face at the center.

Italics

Italic is a lettering style in which the words *slant to the right*. The curious thing about italics is that if, instead of tilting letters to the right, we tilt them to the left, they look much more slanted. Look at the illustration below. The number 7682 was written using the same font seen on many digital clocks and calculator screens and then slanted 15° to left and right. The result is that the number at the left looks more slanted than the right one.

Maybe this is because we are more used to seeing letterings slant to the right, since italics are found in everyday printed material. This can lead us to consider italic a "normal" font, paying no attention to its tilting. We only realize the letter is slanted when we see it tilted in the opposite sense. A simple observation seems to back this theory: if we take figures other than letters, like the parallelogram and the arrow below, and apply the same tilt as above, the left and right slants look tilted by the same degree.

A Luminous Illusion

Ask a friend which side of the box below is darker than the others. He or she will immediately point to the lid. Not so. Place paper strips covering the edges where the lid meets the walls of the box and you'll see they are all the same hue.

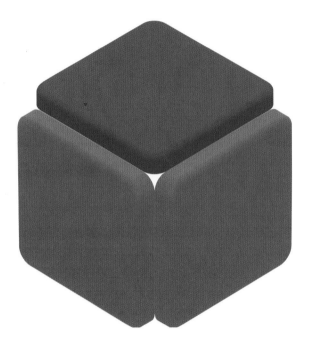

Why is this? It is probably because we compare the hues at the area where the sides meet. If the hues of two nearby areas with the same spatial orientation are identical, then we associate the areas to be alike. The edge of the lid has the same orientation as the walls, but it is slightly darker. Hence, we think the entire lid is darker than the walls.

The Dark Diamonds

This illusion is made up of diamonds. The bottom part of each diamond is darker than the top. All the diamonds are exactly alike. Nevertheless, the diamonds in the top rows look darker than those in the bottom rows. Why? Nobody seems to know for sure.

The Twisted Cord

Cords, strings, telephone cables, and even cables that hold up bridges are all made by twisting together several thinner threads.

This twisting is the source of many perplexing illusions. To produce them, start by painting the individual threads, alternating colored and light strips.

As you can see in the illustration above, the alternation between slanted dark and white areas makes the whole cord look tilted, with the right end higher than the left.

The effect increases if we join the ends of two cords with opposite slants. In the illustration below, the two cords look farther away at the center than at the ends.

This illusion can be applied in many ways; for example, to letters. The strokes forming the word "TILE" are made of horizontal and vertical cords, but it nevertheless looks slanted.

The cords superimposed over the rays in the illusion are perfectly circular. Check it. However, we see them as spirals.

The Size of Heavenly Bodies

Have you ever seen a full Moon rising above the horizon over distant trees or buildings as compared to a full Moon high in the sky? It looks larger closer to the horizon than high up in the sky. But the fact is the Moon is the same size in both instances. You can check it easily.

Make a hole on a piece of paper around a $\frac{1}{4}$ inch ($\frac{1}{2}$ cm) in diameter. Extend your arm and look at the rising Moon through the hole. It will almost match the hole size. Several hours later, when the Moon is high in the sky, repeat the experiment. Again, Moon and hole will almost match, proving that nothing has changed and that the size difference is just an illusion. The origin of this illusion is still a matter of great debate among scientists.

Below is a photograph of the Great Wall of China. Make a photocopy of the picture and draw a Moon or Sun in the sky. What should be its size? Make a guess and then look at the answer on page 119.

Perpetual Motion

The illusion above is based on a painting by French artist Isaia Leviant. Look at the blue rings: some parts seem to be moving all by themselves. What makes them go round? Nobody is really sure. But if you erase the background rays the movement will stop.

The Mountains of the Moon

The above illusion shows a frieze. Notice how the top half of the frieze looks depressed while the bottom half looks raised. The depressed and raised areas are also continuous. How can this be? Where does their difference lie? Not in the color, which is the same in both halves. Nor the shape. The only difference lies in the thin light and dark borders that outline the motifs and give them their depth. In the top half, the darker borders lie above and to the left of the depressed area while the lighter borders lie below and to the right. This scheme is inverted in the bottom half. The borders that lie above and to the left of the raised area are lighter while the darker lie below and to the right.

Why does the different position of dark and light borders make things look either depressed or raised? The answer is that these borders represent light and shadow. The lighter borders represent parts receiving full light and the darker borders represent parts that lie in the shadow. As humans beings, having evolved in a planet where the light comes from the Sun up in the sky, we assume that things are illuminated from above. Hence, if the top part of a figure is lighter and the bottom half is darker, we assume that the figure protrudes. On the other hand, if the top part of a figure is darker and the bottom part is lighter, we assume that the figure recedes. This is easy to check: Go back to the previous page and turn the book upside down. You will see that raised areas now recede and receded areas now protrude.

What about the borders at the sides of the motifs? Do they influence our perception? The next figure shows that they do not. Although the first panel has a lighter border at left and the last panel has it at right, they both look raised. The same holds for the second and third panels: both look depressed.

Our perception based on light and shadow is so strong that it can even modify what we see. The next photo shows an area of the Moon.

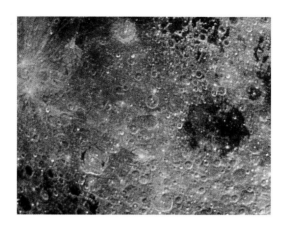

This photo is the same as the last one but turned 180°. If the first were the only photo of the Moon, you would think that, instead of craters, the Moon has mountains.

With all your experience now in light and shadow, try to solve the following puzzle.

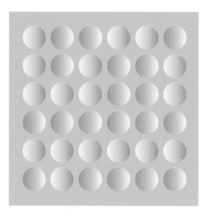

The number 15 is hidden in the above image. Can you find it?

Answer on page 121.

The Christmas Tree

If you look at the illustration above you will notice dark spots appearing and disappearing on the white circles. But if you try to fix your eyes on one of the dark spots, it will immediately disappear. This Christmas tree looks like it has blinking lights.

The Sense of It

"That person is nuts!" "I fed the squirrels some nuts." "She knows the nuts and bolts of this project." All of these sentences have the word "nuts" in common, but it has a very different meaning in each instance: crazy, a hard-shelled seed, and working parts. Its meaning is derived relative to the other words in the sentence.

The next illusion shows that the same can happen when letters and numbers are involved. Depending on how you look at it, the figure in the center has two different meanings. Looking at the numbers above and below, it represents the number 13. Looking at the letters to the left and right of it, it represents the letter B.

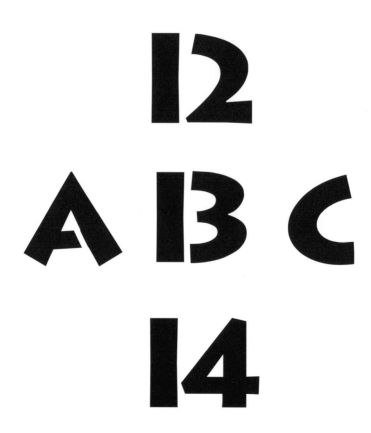

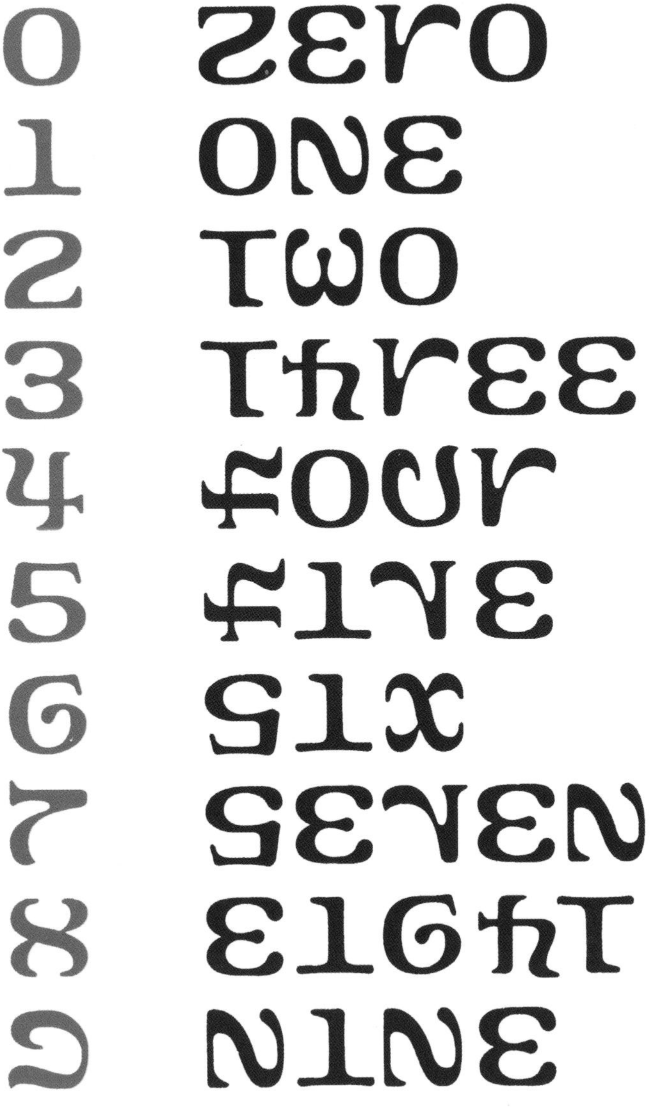

0	ZERO
1	ONE
2	TWO
3	THREE
4	FOUR
5	FIVE
6	SIX
7	SEVEN
8	EIGHT
9	NINE

It is even possible to write complete words from numbers. The above illustration was created by graphic and puzzle artist Scott Kim. The numbers in the left column are used to create the words in the right column.

Even letters inside a word can be seen differently depending upon the word. For example, what do the words below say?
Classic dance.

classic dance

But the same strokes used for the letter "d" of "dance" were used for the letters "cl" of "classic." The reason why we read "classic dance" instead of "dassic clance" is that the words "dassic" and "clance" simply do not exist.

Now, how do you read the next word? Maybe "duster," maybe "cluster." It's hard to say. It depends on which word comes to mind first.

cluster

Here's a final test. What do you read this time? Probably "clear day," maybe even "clear clay."

clear clay

You probably will not read "dear day" or "dear clay." That's because, although the words exist, the combination doesn't make any sense.

The Shadow on the Board

The illustration below shows a ball just a second before it hits the board. It all looks quite normal.

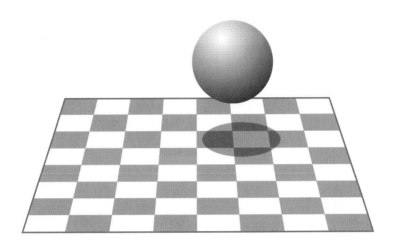

But look at the white square where the ball's shadow is cast. It isn't as white as it looks. As a matter of fact, it has exactly the same hue as the darker squares not in shadow. You can check it by using a piece of paper with a cutout square. Place the opening over the shaded white square as shown below.

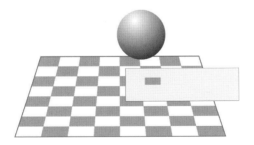

Two things seem to be occurring here. First, our perception recognizes that the white square lies in shadow. (We'll see how we may do this in a later chapter.) Then it automatically adjusts for the difference, making us believe the square is lighter than it really is.

Shady Comparisons

Look at the illustration below. Two squares in different shades of blue—one navy, the other periwinkle—each contain a small orange square. The two orange squares are the same color; however, the one placed over the periwinkle square looks darker. This phenomenon, familiar to scientists and artists, is known as simultaneous contrast.

If you want to verify this illusion as you did before in the previous chapter, take a piece of paper and cut out two square holes so that they will show the orange squares but cover the blue squares. The two orange squares will now look the same.

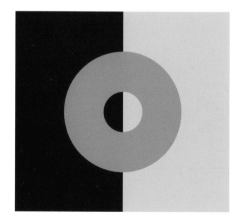

In the illustration at the bottom of the previous page, the different blue backgrounds and orange ring are the same colors as in the previous figure. However, this time the part of the ring lying over the periwinkle does not seem darker than the part over the navy blue. This is because the ring is a continuous surface. The simultaneous contrast illusion actually still exists. If you compare an area on the far left of the ring with an area on the far right, the colors will look quite different. But the continuous surface of the ring causes the increase in the color difference to occur so slowly and gradually that we do not notice it.

If the figure is divided in half and then separated by just a short distance, as below, the contrast illusion reappears.

As a challenge, manipulate the last figure (without coloring it, of course) so that the difference between the colors of the two halves seems to increase even more. This can be done in two ways. One involves cutting the illustration—which will destroy the book! The other way only involves folding the page.

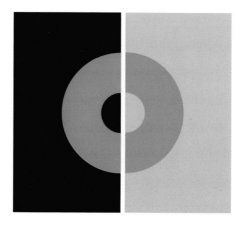

Answer on page 125.

The Dividing Line

What's the difference between these two illustrations below? They are both made up of square tiles, they have the same colors, and their tiles are arranged in the same manner. Nonetheless, the tiles in the bottom illustration look not only sharper but as if they were of different sizes; the yellow tiles look bigger than the blues and the border between rows or columns seems to curve.

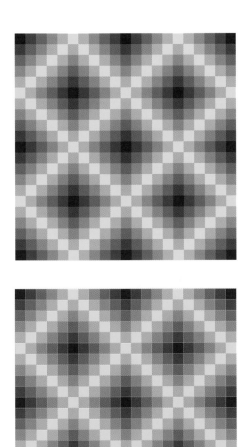

Where does this curving effect come from? If you look closely at the bottom illustration on the previous page, you'll notice one small difference between that and the top illustration: a thin orange line separates the tiles. This line causes the illusion. You can easily see it in the next two illustrations. Both illustrations are made of rectangles, but the rectangles in the bottom illustration seem to have been transformed into wedges by adding lines.

This visual illusion is known as the "coffee wall illusion" because it was first observed on the black and white bricks of a coffee shop wall. The dividing line was the mortar in the joints between bricks. The effect produced by the dividing line is related to the twisted cord illusions on page 20.

The Hand Knows Better

This illusion is from E.B. Titchener. In the two groups of spheres below, the central ones are the same size, but the right one looks larger. The strange fact is that although we see them as different sizes, we somehow know they are not.

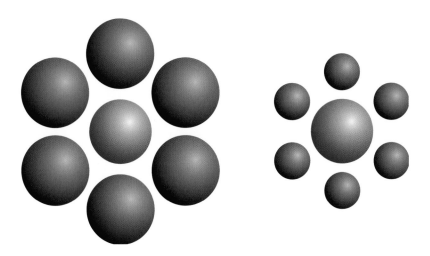

A very simple test demonstrates this. A version of the illusion, with the spheres replaced by round chips, is laid on a desk. Participants are asked to compare the two central chips. They all agree that the right central chip is larger. They are then asked to pick up both central chips. The strange thing is that, while reaching to grab them, the participants opened their hands in exactly the same amount, be it for the right or the left chip. It appears as if, although the eyes tell them one thing, the hand knows better.

Even if the central chips are replaced by other chips, larger or smaller than in the illustration, but are identical in size, the participants open their hands more or less accordingly, but always the same amount for both chips.

Near and Far

What does the illustration on this page show? Just a group of dots in various sizes? Step away from the book and now the points seem to come together and a figure appears: a little duck.

If two adjacent objects are close to us, then we can see them in greater detail and as separate entities. However, if the two objects are further away, then their distinction becomes less clear. When we look closely at the little duck, we see the individual dots. When we step back from the illustration, our eyes cannot see the dots as acutely. Therefore, we merge them into the continuous shape of a duck.

Some eyes are better than others: the eyes of falcons and other predatory birds have greater acuity than ours. They can detect small animals, like rodents, from thousands of feet away. They can see the individual dots in the duck illustration from farther away than we humans.

All illustrated books are based on our relative lack of separation power. Look at a full color illustration under a magnifying glass. You'll notice two things. One, only four color printing inks are used: yellow, a greenish-blue called cyan, a reddish-purple called magenta, and black. Two, the colors aren't always continuous. Like the toy duck, they are composed of evenly spaced dots that are bigger where the color is stronger and smaller where lighter. This arrangements of dots is called the "printing screen." The idea is to use a screen with dots so near each other that our eyes cannot separate them. This forces our perception to merge them and see the figure as a whole. As merging the dots also implies merging their

colors, a certain hue—for example, a green—is made by merging nearby blue and yellow dots.

The illustrations in these pages make use of this. But, this time, the figures are not made of dots, but of other figures. Look closer and you'll see the smaller figures. Step back and you'll see the complete scene. The head of "*Le Clown Songeur* (Thoughtful Clown)," a painting by French artist André Martins de Barros, is made of female bodies while two musicians account for Shakespeare's face in the poster by Hungarian graphic artist István Orosz.

Seeing Ghosts

If you were asked to describe the illusion below, you would probably say it was a white square over four blue blotches. The problem is the square does not exist. The borders are incomplete. Only the four corners are well defined. And yet we keep seeing the square and even perceive its color to be somewhat brighter than the color of the page. Again, this is not so: if you scan the illustration with a photometer (a device that measures the quantity of light similar to the one photographic cameras have) no difference between the square and the surrounding white paper will be found.

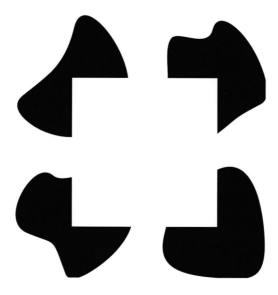

The next illusion is another way of showing the square. Now you can see the blue blotches though some parts are lighter, as if a tinted square was placed over these sections. The sense of a tinted material existing is so strong that the lighter blue parts seem to diffuse out and tint the empty space between the corners. So a ghost light-blue square, with complete borders separating it from the white paper, is perceived.

Scientists have a theory to explain why we see things that don't exist. They say that when we see an incomplete figure, our brain interprets the missing part as hidden by some object. The white square and the light blue square are the objects in these two illusions. Seeing ghost figures is the way our brain puts them into existence. In fact, our brain not only creates a nonexistent object, but it also assigns it a color.

Some may ask: What is an "incomplete figure"? Or, to put it the other way, when is a figure "complete"? Although this isn't easy to define, the following illustration demonstrates the idea. The central part of the two figures shows a sort of flattened circle. But in the left figure, this flattened circle is perceived as a ghost figure while in the right figure it is not.

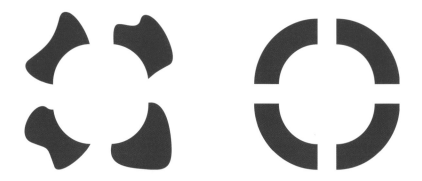

Following what we said, the blotches of the left illustration should be "incomplete" while those of the right illustration should be "complete." The green parts of the left illustration have been smoothly and logically carved out. But the green parts in the right illustration have also been similarly carved. So where does the difference lie?

The difference is that in the right figure the curved cuts are parallel to the exterior border of the green parts. This parallelism is what makes a figure look complete.

Although parallelism is a good indication of completeness, sometimes it isn't enough. The three illustrations below show variations on this theme. In the left illustration, a ghost square covers a part of four concentric squares. (Notice how the square shape overrides the parallelism.) In the middle illustration, the ghost square does not appear, but there are small ghost rectangles in the gaps of the borders. In the right illustration, there is no ghost figure. Each one of the L shapes is perceived as a complete figure.

Turn the Lights Off!

In the illusion below, a blue disk seems to be glowing in the center. Resembling the ghost figures in the previous chapter, the blue lines seem to spread over the paper to create a ghost circle.

Tip: If you cannot see the disk, step back from the book or look at it with eyes half shut.

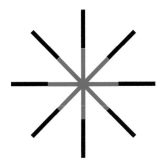

This illusion is known as "neon illumination" because the effect produced is similar to that with neon light signs.

The next illusion seems to have a red diamond inside a square black grid. The effect is so strong that you have to look closer to see that the diamond is only made of lines and that the red background is an illusion.

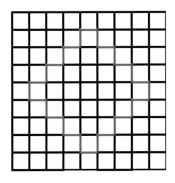

This next illustration is a variation on an illusion in the previous chapter. Now, the neon effect not only spreads between the green lines, but a ghost square can be seen as if a green filter is present. Finally, a phantom road is paved with blue neon illusions.

Now that you know how to turn on neon lights, your task is to turn them off. Going back to the first illustration, how can you remove the glow without erasing the whole figure? The answer isn't as straight as it looks. For example, if you remove the blue lines, the center of the figure will still have a glow that looks brighter than the paper surrounding it.

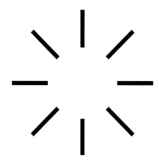

Answer on page 118.

The Long, Long Lizard

Suppose you see a car parked behind a tree. The front and the rear of the car are clearly visible but the middle is hidden by the tree trunk. Since you can't see behind the tree, for all you know, instead of one car, there could well be just two parts of a car with the tree hiding the gap. But, no matter how hard you try, you cannot imagine a car divided into two separate pieces. Why?

Some scientists think the completion of forms follows certain rules. One of them states that we perceive a continuous object when the extension of the surfaces of the parts at both sides of the covered object meet smoothly, and the volume enclosed by these surfaces can merge. The rule is so strong that, although we know lizards aren't this long, instead of imagining two animals, we cannot avoid seeing but one winding around the barber pole.

Hide and Seek

Hidden figures were very popular in the 19th century. The idea was simple: a card was printed with a seemingly normal illustration of, say, a landscape. But hidden in the landscape were objects or persons that were not perceptible at first sight. The viewer had to discover them.

This form of entertainment was used in France with political undertones. The illustration above shows a bouquet of violets. If you study it carefully you will discover three hidden profiles: under the outer petal of the top left flower is a female profile looking to the right; under the top right leaf is a male profile looking to the left; and in the middle is a child profile looking to the right. For Frenchmen of the times the meaning was quite clear. The profiles belonged to Napoleon, who was then in exile with his wife and son. The violets were there to remind the viewer that Napoleon had sworn to be back by the season when violets flowered.

The following illustration was made by Mitsumasa Anno, a great Japanese graphic artist. At initial sight, the illustration seems to show a woodland scene. But hidden in the foliage are two elephants, a camel, a pig, two rabbits, a cat, an eagle, an anteater, a boar, and a baboon. Can you find them?

Answer on page 124.

Arrowheads

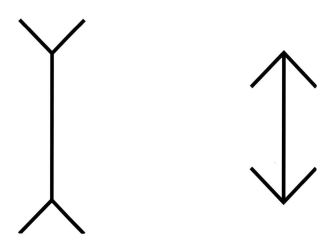

Which of the two vertical lines placed between the arrowheads is longer, the one at left with the arrows pointing inward or the one at right with the arrows pointing outward? Although both have the same length, the one at left looks longer.

Many scientists think this illusion occurs because we associate the arrowheads for wall corners: the figure with inward-pointing arrows represents a concave corner; the one with outward-pointing arrows represents a convex corner. Usually, when we look at a wall of constant height, concave corners are farther away than convex corners and, hence, project a smaller image on the retina. But, as we know both corners have the same height, a process called "size constancy" in our brain automatically adjusts for the difference and enlarges our perception of concave corners.

But if both corners are drawn the same height, as in the above illustration, the size constancy mechanism is still at work and we perceive the corner that normally will be farther away (the one at the left) higher than it really is.

Let's check this theory by comparing the corner heights in a drawing of a wall.

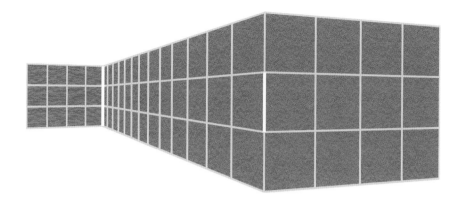

In the above illustration, a brick in the nearest corner (indicated with a white line) has the same height as the whole far corner (also indicated in white). Nonetheless, the distant corner looks much longer. Notice how the joints between bricks and the white lines make arrowhead figures similar to those in the first illusion.

The Ponzo illusion below seems to work in a similar way. In the left figure, the top red line looks longer than the bottom red line. We might be thinking that the slanted lines are actually parallel, as in a real landscape like the road in the right photograph. Again, the size constancy mechanism adjusts our perception of the lines: Believing the upper line to be farther away, the brain automatically enlarges it.

Tiles and Chessboard

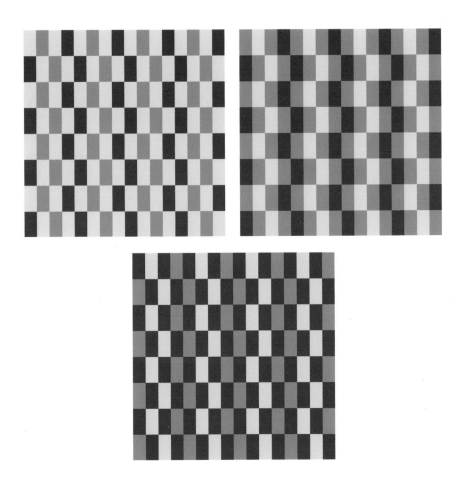

The three illustrations above follow a similar pattern. All three are made of small rectangles in three shades of brown. In the first illustration, a medium brown and dark brown rectangle alternate between two light brown rectangles. In the second illustration, a light brown and dark brown rectangle alternate between two medium brown rectangles. In the last illustration, a light brown and medium brown rectangle alternate between two dark brown rectangles. Then why do we perceive the second illustration as being different? Were you to describe the three, you'd probably say the first and last are made of rectangular tiles, while the second looks like a chessboard with checkered columns.

A chessboard has only two colors. Where does the extra color come from? The vertical lines of dark and medium brown are perceived as a shadow casted on. For example, this illustration can represent a wall with light and medium brown tiles upon which some columns cast their shadow. In the places where the shadows fall, the colors are seen as darker: the light brown is transformed into medium brown and the medium brown into dark brown.

In the Making of Mist chapter (see page 100), we will see what colors an object has to be in order to be perceived as being partially in shadow, even if the object that casts the shadow is not seen.

Building Makeovers

Make-up and cosmetics have been used since the time of Babel and Pharaoh's Egypt. Some types of cosmetics, like lipstick or mascara, are used to enhance existing features. Others are used to create nonexistent features, like alien faces in the science fiction shows.

American artist Richard Haas is a specialist in this latter kind of make-up, only, instead of putting make-up on faces, he applies it to buildings. The photograph below shows one of his works. The windows, cornices, and pilasters are not really there. They, and the shadows they cast, were painted over the naked wall. The original building is on the next page. Compare both photos to see which of the features are real and which are created by Haas. Notice the building was somewhat modified; the false gables that crown the walls are new and intended to relate the building to the other nearby building.

Another wonderful example of building makeover is the Unicorn Cottage at Pormeirion, Wales, designed by Sir Clough Williams-Ellis. Seen from the front, the cottage looks like a two-story house in Edwardian style.

But seen from the back, its true nature is revealed: the house has only one story. Since the house lies at the top of a ravine, the front is seen from below to enhance the deception.

Floating Diamonds

If you look at the illustration below for a while you'll notice some strange things occurring. At first, it only looks like a group of lines. Suddenly, the lines seem to organize themselves into two diamond shapes, one inside the other. Sometimes the smaller diamond seems to float above the bigger, but an instant later, maybe after you blink, the smaller diamond seems to recede and the bigger advances toward you.

As an experiment, while looking at the figure, try to focus your eyes so that these two positions shift.

Visual Turbine

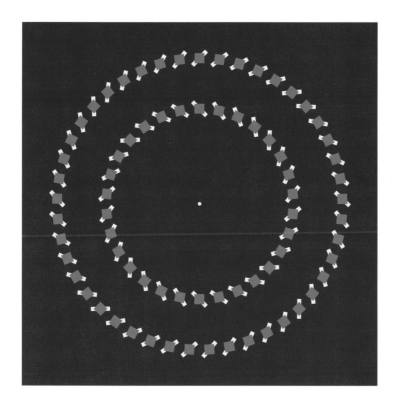

Hydroelectric dams produce energy by making a current of water flow through the slanted blades of a turbine. The water pushes the blades and the turbine spins. From a mechanical point of view, a water turbine transforms a straight motion into a rotational one. Here you'll do the same but, instead of water, you'll use your eyes.

Place the book at reading distance, look directly at the central dot and slowly move your head forward and backward. The circles will spin in opposite directions—in one sense when you move forward and in the opposite sense when you move backward. If you can't make it work the first time, try placing the book at different distances. And don't forget to look at the dot.

The Movements of the Eyes

Bring the book to eye level and fix your gaze on the smudge below. Make sure not to blink or move your eyes. After a little time (be patient), the smudge will disappear. If you keep looking, it might suddenly reappear only to disappear once more.

Once you've gotten enough practice making the smudge fade away, go to the next page and try to make that smudge disappear. This time, no matter how much you try, it will not disappear.

What is the difference between the two smudges? In the Hole in the Eye chapter (see page 14), we said that our retinas are covered by cells that get activated when they receive light. The curious thing about these cells is that, if they keep on receiving the same amount of light, they will deactivate all by themselves. In other words, the cells are active only when the amount of light they receive changes. This changing in the amount of light received is what usually happens when we look, since the scene we see with our eyes is constantly changing. Also, when we blink, the cells in our retinas do not receive light for an instant, hence, refreshing the image. In addition to these relatively large movements, the eyes are constantly making little involuntary movements that resemble a tremor, which are only seen through precise laboratory equipment.

In the first illustration, the smudge has diffuse borders and the darkness gradually makes a smooth transition to lightness. When we gaze at it without blinking, the eyes only move involuntarily. But these little movements can only go from a point of the image to a neighboring one that has almost the same color. As there are no changes in the amount of light received, the cells in the retina deactivate and the image disappears. On the other hand, the smudge in the second illustration has an abrupt change in color at the white ring. This change is enough to activate the cells when the eye makes its involuntary movements.

The Hollow Bone

The work above was painted in 1533 by Hans Holbein, *the Younger* (not to be confused with his father, *the Older*, who was also a painter). The painting is called "The Ambassadors" and it is the portrait of two Frenchmen carrying out a diplomatic mission at the English court of Henry VIII.

The portrait was commissioned by the man at the left. He and his friend are surrounded by objects depicting their interests: astronomical

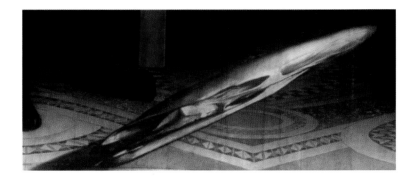

and musical instruments, mathematical books, clocks, musical scores, and a globe. But what is the elongated object diagonally across the bottom of the picture? Enlarging it (see above), it looks like nothing recognizable.

Let's imagine that the object is painted on a stretched-out piece of some elastic material. Let go of the top right and bottom left corner. When the material contracts, the unexpected result will be the one below.

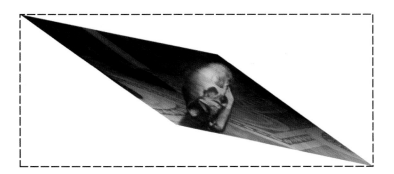

The next question is: What is a skull doing there? And why did Holbein distort it? Let's start with the second question. Suppose the painting hung in a big hall, some 8 or 10 feet above the ground. From almost any place in the room it will be seen as we see it at the beginning of this chapter. But if somebody approached it from a bottom-left angle, he or she will clearly see the skull. This could happen if, for example, a flight of stairs ran along the wall where the portrait hung. Climbing up the stairs and looking up at the painting, the person will notice that a skull had unexpectedly appeared. You can reproduce the situation by looking at the portrait from the direction shown below.

Holbein was not the first to use this type of controlled distortion, called "anamorphosis" in a painting. Leonardo da Vinci studied anamorphoses a few decades before him. We can only guess at the reason why

Holbein included a skull. Some think that it relates to the man who commissioned the painting: he wears a hat pin with a skull in it. Others think the skull is there to remind us of the transitory nature of wealth and honor. But the most amusing theory is that the words *holhle bein*, which mean "hollow bone" in German, are pronounced almost like the name Holbein. Therefore, the skull, a hollow bone, might be the artist's way of signing the painting.

Impossible Shapes

The illusion shows some flights of stairs seen from below. At first glance, everything looks quite normal, but if you try to follow the flights all sort of odd things happen. It is clear that all the floor around the staircase is level. However, if you enter the stairs from the top left, you must climb two steps to reach the central landing, but descend only one to exit through the opposite side. If you enter from the bottom left, you must first descend two steps to reach the landing and climb one to exit through the opposite side. Or, if you enter from the top left, climb the two steps up to the landing and try to exit through the bottom left stairs, you must still climb two more steps. How can all this be? To understand it, let's first see how this type of figure is constructed.

Imagine a structure like a construction scaffolding. The scaffoldings are placed evenly distanced in all directions to form cubic divisions.

Now, let's draw a part of the structure (bottom left) and a closed figure along some of the scaffolding.

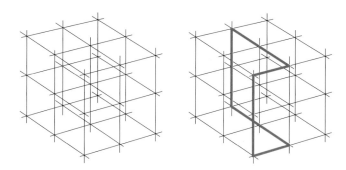

Let's substitute the scaffolding with square-section bars. This can be done in the three different ways shown below. But if we were to try to make these, we could only make the left one. The other two drawings represent objects that are impossible to construct. One can even say these drawings are a mistake. In the middle figure, the horizontal bar, instead of being behind, intersects the vertical bar. In the right figure, the horizontal bar is in front.

Some artists purposely incorporate these "mistakes" in their work to achieve unexpected effects, like the flights of stairs at the beginning of this chapter. Being impossible to construct, these objects are known as *impossible figures* or *impossible objects*.

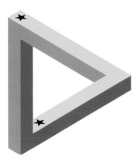

The best known impossible object is the impossible triangle. We have just seen one at the lower part of the middle figure in the previous illusion. The impossible triangle above shows the illusion on a larger scale. Let's study it. Following the yellow horizontal bar, both stars lie at the same level. But following the vertical bar, a star winds up above the other. This paradox is the result of considering two points that lie at different distances as matching.

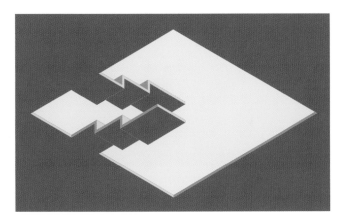

Let's go back to the staircase illusion at the beginning of this chapter. Above, you can see the two left flights, but this time they are drawn as they really are with the descending flight passing below the ascending one (the same can be done with the right staircases). As with the impossible triangle, to get an impossible staircase you must take two steps that lie at different heights and make them a single step.

M.C. Escher was the best known artist to use impossible figures. His work can be found in many places, so we aren't going to include it here. Instead, we will see how to build an impossible figure.

The first method is based on what we have already seen: two different points that are depicted as a single point. The photograph below, taken by Bruno Ernst, a mathematician who was a friend of Escher, shows it quite clearly. As you can see in the mirror, the seemingly impossible triangle is really an open figure. What transforms it into an impossible object is the point of view chosen by Ernst to take the photograph (more on this in Seeing with Two Eyes; see page 85).

The second method is quite different. The sculpture on the next page is called *Unity*. It is located at the center of the Belgium town where the author, Mathieu Hamaekers, lives. Again, this is an impossible triangle standing on one of its corners.

But if you walk around to the side of the sculpture, you'll discover that it isn't impossible at all. It is an absolutely possible triangle with curved limbs. As happened with the Ernst photograph, the figure looks impossi-

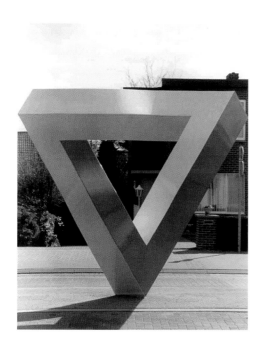

ble only when seen from a certain angle.

Now that we know impossible figures are not impossible but merely illusions created by seeing them from a certain angle, let's return to the staircase at the beginning of the chapter. Here is an interesting paradox: instead of seeing a possible construction made of twisted staircases, we keep on seeing an impossible figure. Between choosing curved steps and a staircase full of climbing paradoxes, we prefer the latter. Our perception is a curious thing: it deceives itself. Even worse, it deceives itself while having complete knowledge of the deception.

Probably the best explanation of this paradox is what scientists call the "generic view" assumption. When looking at a scene, our perception considers the view to be ordinary. If we move slightly, the scene will not change. Applied to impossible figures this means we assume that two points which coincide in the view will also match in reality, or that a straight line will still be straight when looked at from another angle. Ernst's photograph and the first view of Hamaekers' *Unity* were carefully designed to fool the generic view assumption.

The Third Pole

Bring the opposite page parallel to the floor and up to chin level, about 4 or 5 inches (10 or 13 cm) away from your face.

Look with both eyes at the place where the poles cross. Suddenly a third pole will appear between the two, vertically and with the same bands of color.

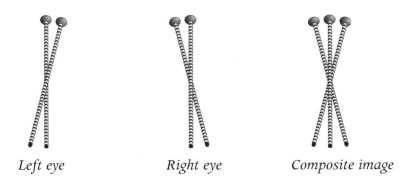

| *Left eye* | *Right eye* | *Composite image* |

Where does the third pole come from? Bring the book again to chin level. One of the poles will point directly to one eye and the other pole to the other eye. Now, taking care not to move the book, alternately open and close your eyes. The pole pointing to your open eye will look straight while the other will appear even more slanted than in the book. When you look with both eyes, your brain composes an image from both poles. The middle pole is that image composed. The side poles are the images of the poles not pointing at the eyes (the ones that look more slanted). When looking with your left eye, the straight pole passes under the other pole. When looking with your right eye, the straight pole passes above the other pole. In the composed image, the central pole sometimes appears above and sometimes below, or even shifts positions while you are looking.

Inward and Outward

This is an easy experiment. Fold a paper in half lengthwise and stand it up on edge like an open book.

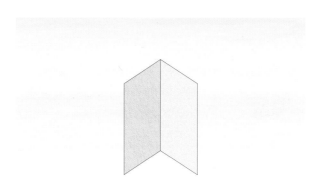

Staring at the crease line, try to invert the fold from a concave (valley) fold to a convex (mountain) fold, like a gable roof. To make this clear, imagine a chess king placed inside the paper fold. You must pass from the left positioning to the right one. With a little practice, you'll be able to shift easily from one position to the other.

What if, somehow, you could make half of the fold into a mountain while the other half remained a valley?

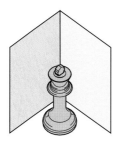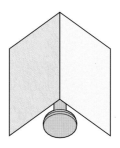

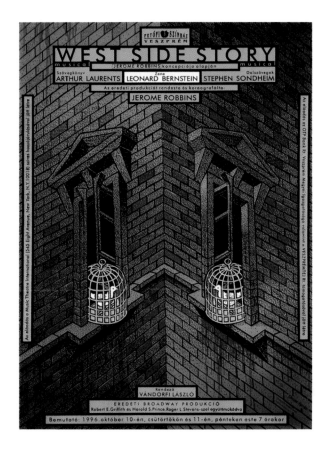

That is exactly what Hungarian artist István Orosz achieved in this poster designed to announce the play version of *West Side Story*. At the top, the corner made by the walls advances outward. At the bottom, it recedes inward. Based on Shakespeare's *Romeo and Juliet*, the play tells the story of two lovers belonging to enemy gangs. The idea is masterfully rendered. While the lovers look at each other (the caged birds), the gangs they belong to turn their backs to each other (the upper part of the windows). Notice how the left wall is illuminated at the top and in shadows at the bottom, while the right wall is illuminated at the bottom and in shadows at the top. This inverse shading scheme stresses the concave and convex effects of the corner while maintaining a coherence with a unique source of light.

Pushing Dots

Suppose there is a black and white checkered tablecloth laid out over a table. You pick it from the center and lift it slightly. Folds will appear and the squares in the pattern will be distorted. The illustration below, based on a work by Japanese scientist A. Kitaoka, may be a good approximation to what the tablecloth would look like.

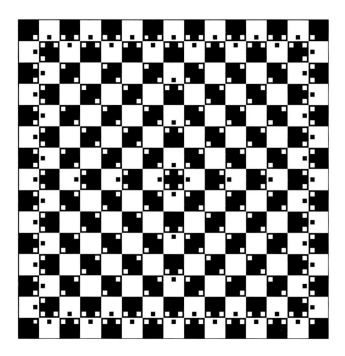

The strange thing is the illustration is not distorted at all. The squares are still squares, the horizontal and vertical lines are not slanted, parallels remain parallel, and straight lines remain straight. You can check this with a ruler. So, what makes them look so distorted? Answer: the little black and white square dots placed near the borders of the larger squares.

In a way, these little square dots seem to push the borders and distort them. These dots can be strategically placed to produce different effects.

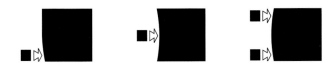

A square dot pushes what is bordering it, displacing it. A dot placed near a corner displaces the corner; a dot placed near the middle displaces the middle; two dots placed near the corners displace the two corners. To our perception, the border looks indented, which affects the neighboring square. The square over which the dot lies expands (the white squares in the first illustration) while its neighbor contracts (the black squares).

Two dots facing exactly opposite each other cancel each other out so that there is no distortion. If they are not exactly facing, then the distortion increases.

How does all this work on a square? See the next illustration: a dot placed near a corner stretches it out; two dots in opposite corners turn the square into a rhombus; three dots at three corners stretch the square so that only one angle seems to remain unaffected.

In the next illustration, four white dots placed outside the white square's border contract the square. A somewhat lesser effect is obtained by placing four black dots inside at the corners. If black and white dots are added the effect increases. Four black dots placed at the inner borders of the white square seems to curve them and expand the square. The expanding increases when surrounding the square with white dots placed at the corners of the neighboring squares. Again, the added action of black and white dots further increases the expansion.

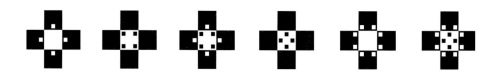

Now that you know everything about the pushing dots, try to solve the following puzzle. Draw black dots near the borders of some white squares in the chessboard below so that it will end up looking like a dome or bubble top.

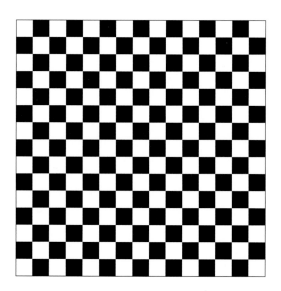

Answer on page 123.

Gravity Lens

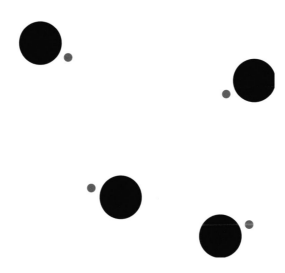

If you were to connect the red dots in the above illustration, what four-sided figure would you get?

Maybe nothing—just an irregular figure like the one below? Actually, this irregular figure is just an illusion. It is actually a parallelogram: a figure with parallel opposite sides, as can be seen on the next page.

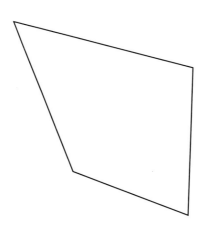

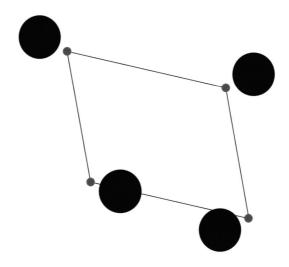

It is easy to see that the blue circles are the source of the illusion. If you cover them with pieces of white paper, then the dots are immediately seen as the vertices of a parallelogram. Somehow, the blue circles seem to visually "attract" the red dots, hence the name "gravity lens."

If you enlarge the circles up to a certain size, the illusion increases. After that, further enlargement actually diminishes the illusion. The illusion also diminishes if you move the dots away from the circles, or if you place the dots so that the sides of the parallelogram are vertical or horizontal.

There are many ways of removing the illusion without removing the disks. For example, if dots and disks are placed in pairs along a straight line, as seen at the top of the next page. Here, the parallel sides also become evident.

Another way of removing the illusion is drawing just a pair of opposite sides of the parallelogram. These sides do not need to go through the dots; it's enough for them to be close by. This effect is seen in the last illustration on the next page.

Can you make the illusion reappear by altering this last figure? You are not allowed to erase or cover any part of it. You can only add new lines

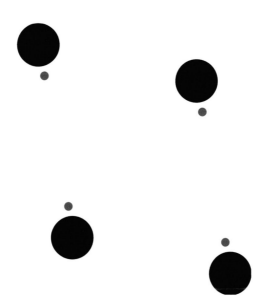

or shapes. When you have finished your drawing, the result will obvi-
ously be different from the first illustration in this chapter, but the gravity lens illusion should be noticeable again.

   HINT: Use a ruler.

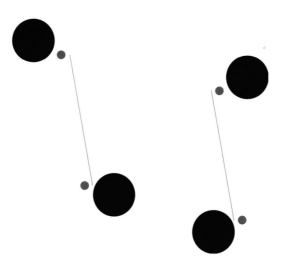

Answer on page 122.

Distorted Buildings

If you travel to Rome, you can check out for yourself some beautiful buildings that contain optical illusions. In the heart of the city, two minutes away from Campo dei Fiori, is Palazzo Spada, an antique residence that is now an art gallery. In 1635, the owner ordered Francesco Borromini, a famous architect and sculptor, to build a colonnade, a gallery flanked by columns. Through the door of one of the residence halls, you enter into a small interior courtyard. At the opposite end of the courtyard appears the colonnade shown in the photograph. The feeling is of depth: the colonnade seems to be 90 or 100 feet (27 or 30 m) long. But that is only an illusion: the actual figure is less than 30 feet (9 m).

How does this illusion work? We are so used to tunnel walls being parallel and the ceiling to be of a constant height that we take it for granted. We don't expect Borromini's colonnade to be different. But that is the way it is: the width and height of the gallery diminishes as you walk through. At the same time, the columns get shorter and are placed nearer each other. The result is a striking optical illusion. As it is based on perspective laws (a system used to draw faithful rendering of objects developed in Italy more than a century before the colonnade was built), it is known as Borromini's *prospettiva*.

An amusing experiment is to place two persons of the same height at the entrance and exit of the colonnade. The person at the exit looks huge. The illusion is so strong that although we know the real size of both persons, instead of a distorted gallery, our perception prefers to see a giant.

Some years before Borromini's perspective, Vincenzo Scamozzi designed the stage decoration for the Olympian Theatre at Vicenza, also in Italy. The façade of the stage has three doors through which city buildings made of wood are seen.

To place a whole city within the inner scene Scamozzi resorted to the same trick as Borromini: streets grow increasingly narrower and buildings become smaller. Of course, the actors never enter the backstage city, unless they are transformed into giants in the play so that the illusion becomes evident.

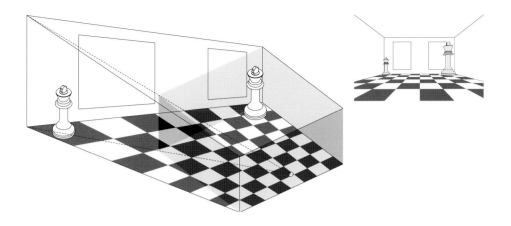

The Ames room is a specially constructed room that employs this distorted illusion. The children in the facing page are the same height but the room is distorted. This is how it works.

In the illustration above, the gray box shows an undistorted room. The checkerboard floor and the distorted walls show the actual room. The white dot in the front wall is a hole through which the scene is observed. From that point, the corners of the undistorted box and the distorted room lie on the same line of sight. This means they both project the same image in the retina and the eye perceives the actual room as undistorted. But, on the other hand, as the king placed at the left corner is farther away than the one at the right corner (but at the same distance from the back wall), one perceives it as being much smaller.

However, the effect seems not to be due exclusively to the shape of the room: if you get rid of everything but the children and the base of the back wall from the photo, the illusion, although somewhat weakened, still works.

Only One Head

The curious illustration above is a Japanese stamp created by Yamamoto Hisabei in 1835 known as "Five Heads, Ten Children." The title is self-explanatory: every two bodies share a head (and the arms or legs). For example, the two children below share their heads, shoulders, and arms.

The same illusion was already used in the 12th century in a Persian dish, but with three horses sharing a head. Study carefully the dish and then try to solve the following puzzle created by Sam Loyd. Photocopy the illustration below and cut it along the dotted lines. Then rearrange the pieces so the jockeys ride two galloping horses.

Answer on page 119.

Suns and Black Holes

In the Seeing Ghosts chapter (see page 40), we made ghost figures appear. In that chapter, all the figures had well-defined borders; in this one, the ghost figures will seem to radiate.

Take the illusion below. The center seems to radiate from a light of its own, whiter that the white on the paper. It looks like the Sun. There are no well-defined borders and the rays seem to diffuse into the background.

The effect also works with the negative of the figure, although this time, instead of a Sun, the illusion looks like a black hole with the dark center that is darker than the black background.

The next illusion represents a sort of transition between the Sun and the ghost figures in the Seeing Ghosts chapter. The lines have small steps, creating the illusion of a series of concentric circles, ranging from a bright center to the paper background. The right figure shows how the circles are formed.

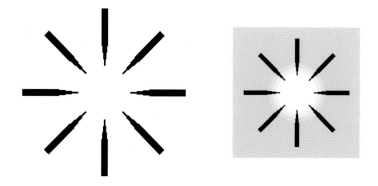

Extra Columns

The columns below have a strange characteristic: there are four columns in the top half but only three in the bottom. The reason is that somewhere along its length the fronts of some columns that looked forward began to look sideways and vice versa. The color gradation is specially intended to conceal the changes in orientation.

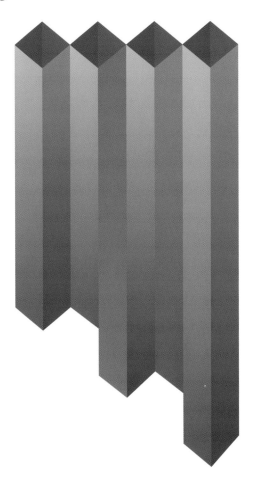

A little puzzle. The illusion of columns includes an optical illusion that has nothing to do with its impossibility, but with the colors of its faces. Can you find it?

Answer on page 123.

Seeing with Two Eyes

The distance between an adult person's two eyes is some 2.5 or 3 inches (6.25 or 7.5 cm). As a result, each eye sees a somewhat different image. The brain uses this difference to gather information on the distance and depth of an object it could not get from one eye only. Let's see how it works.

In the chapter on impossible shapes (see page 61), we saw a photograph of an impossible object that wasn't impossible at all. The photograph was taken with a camera, so it can be considered as the view of only one eye. What would happen if the impossible triangle were to be seen with both eyes? For the right eye, points A (the top of the vertical bar with the word "SUMATRA") and B (the right tip of the horizontal bar with the word "ORIGINEEL") coincide to form the impossible triangle. But for the left eye, these points don't match; it sees that point B is behind point A. The brain gets the information from both images and deduces that the triangle is made by three bars that do not make up a closed figure. This is the principle of stereo vision, and in this chapter we'll use it to trick the brain into believing that a plane image has three dimensions.

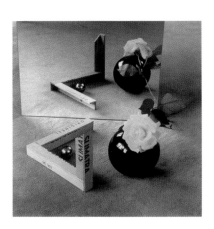

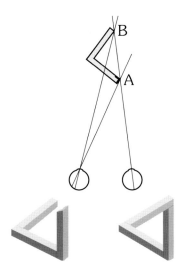

Remember how you created an extra pole in The Third Pole chapter (see page 66)? We'll use a similar method to get depth from plane figures similar to those popularized years ago in *The Magic Eye* books. Scientists call these types of images "stereograms."

Let's start with the above illustration. Lift it to eye level and draw it close to your face while focusing your eyes on a distant point beyond the book. Don't try to focus on the illustration. At any moment, as happened with the poles, the two disks will turn into three like the image below.

Without losing sight of the three disks, slowly move the book away from your face up to your usual reading distance. What you've done is to look at each disk with a different eye so that the left disk is the image of the left disk seen with the left eye, the right disk is the image of the right disk seen with the right eye, and the disk in the middle is a composite of the disks seen by both eyes—exactly what you did with the two poles.

Now, do the same with the beetles and butterflies on the next page. Try to merge the center beetles by looking at each one with an eye. Slowly, move the book away. At a reading distance, you will see five beetles and five butterflies floating in the air. Notice that the beetles are closer to you than the butterflies.

Why are they at different distances? Since the technique works by making two different objects merge into one image, if the objects are farther apart, the eyes will merge them farther away than if the objects were closer together. You can see it in the next illustration. The merging of the two beetles images is closer to the eyes than the merging of the two butterflies images.

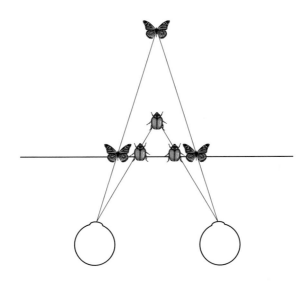

A variation of this technique is the random dot stereogram created by Bela Julesz. In these stereograms, instead of a recognizable object, each eye receives the image of a group of dots. In the illustration below, two similar groups of dots are arranged in a square (indicated by a white line). Notice how the right square is somewhat displaced over the background. When you merge the images, the square is perceived as floating. Of course, instead of a square the dots can be other shapes.

Images can be hidden in a background. This is the most common type of stereogram. In the image below, leaves were used instead of dots to form square tiles that you must merge as before. If you look at it long enough, you will then see a cone emerging from a round hole.

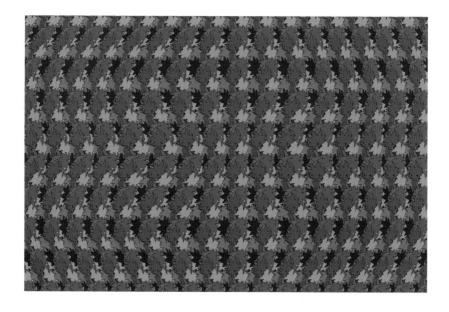

Erecting Obelisks

How did ancient Egyptians erect their one-stone block obelisks that weigh dozens of tons? Archeologists have different theories. Here you'll be able to achieve this feat without any effort except the power of your eyes. Close one eye, place the other near the triangle at the bottom of the page, and lean the book back. At any moment, the obelisks will be erected all by themselves.

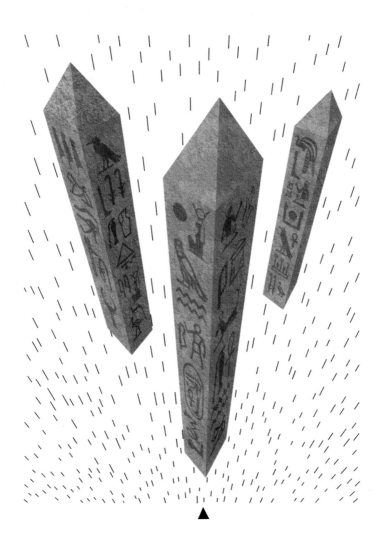

Looking Through the Window

To see these illusions, you must use the stereogram technique mentioned in the Seeing with Two Eyes chapter (see page 85). When it becomes three-dimensional, the illusion below shows four circular windows through which a black background and a red board that bends backward is seen. The region between windows (the white paper) is well defined and hides part of the red board.

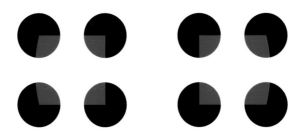

If we now change part of the illusion so that the part seen with the left eye is now seen with the right eye, and vice versa, something odd happens. See the illusion below. The red board now bends forward. But there's more: the circular windows are no longer windows but black disks placed over the paper. And even more: the red board is transformed into a lighter red ghost figure that tints the space in between the disks.

All these changes happened simply because we looked at something first with one eye and then with the other!

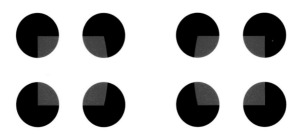

Contrast Adjustment

Just like television sets, our eyes have a contrast adjustment system. But, instead of a knob or button, our system adjusts itself automatically. It is mainly used to detect lines. How? Look at the borders between any two of the gray bands. At each side of the border, the color looks different than in the rest of the band: lighter over the light bar and darker over the dark bar. Actually, these hue differences do not exist. They're just a trick of our perception to increase the contrast between neighboring bands and, hence, emphasize the dividing line.

This effect originates in the light sensitive cells of the eyes' retina. The cells are interconnected, making several different systems. One of these systems is what scientists call "lateral inhibition." Its function is to analyze and modify data gathered by other systems when light enters the eye. Neighboring cells in a lateral inhibition system are interconnected. A cell receiving light sends a signal to the brain. At the same time, the connected cells send to the brain opposite signals that counteract or inhibit the signal sent by the first cell. The following diagram shows how it works. The numbers are arbitrary and merely used to demonstrate the system.

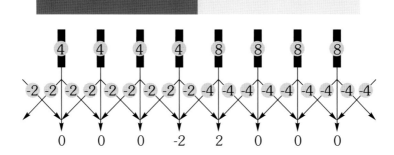

The upper band shows two neighboring areas, one a light gray, the other a dark gray. These could be, for example, two bands in the previous illustration. Below the bands is a row of black vertical rectangles with a disk and a number in each. These represent some cells in the retina interconnected in a lateral inhibition scheme, and the number stands for the amount of light it receives. Hence, cells looking at the dark gray band receive less light (4) than cells looking at the light gray (8). Cells are interconnected in such a way that the value sent to the brain is the value of the light received by a cell minus half the value received by each neighboring cell. For example, the second cell from the left receives a light value of 4. From this figure, a value of 2 from the neighboring cell at the left and a value of 2 from the neighbor at the right must be subtracted. Then, the result transmitted to the brain is 0, or nothing. This means that the lateral inhibition system working on the second cell from the left tells the brain not to modify the data obtained by other systems at the point of the scene the cell is looking at.

If you study the above illustration you can see that, as long as the gray band doesn't change color, the system keeps on sending zero values. But something quite different happens with cells at each side of the border between bands. The cell looking at the dark gray receives a value of 4. As the value from its neighboring left cell is 2, and the value from its right neighbor is 4, the final value transmitted to the brain is 4 − 2 − 4. Result: −2. In a similar way, the cell that looks at the light gray receives a value of 8. As the value of its neighboring left cell is 2, and its neighboring right cell is 4, are subtracted, the result is 2. That is, the lateral inhibition system tells the brain to add a darker band (−2) at one side of the border and a lighter band (2) at the other side. Along the rest of the band, no modifications should be made (0).

One of the many simplifications in the previous diagram is that the cells were placed in only one row. Our retinas, however, cover not a line but a surface, so the cells do not have only two neighbors; they are surrounded by other cells. The arrangement of cells in a lateral inhibition system over a surface is called a "receptive field."

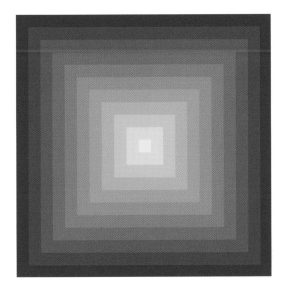

The illustration above shows lateral inhibition working on a surface. The illustration is made of a series of frames placed one inside the other in the order of darker to lighter. The hue in each frame is even; there are no gradations. Nonetheless, four luminous rays can be seen going from the center out through the corners of the illustration. These rays are an illusion. You can check by looking with a magnifier or by covering sections with pieces of paper.

How does lateral inhibition work on a surface? Below, the left illustration shows a very simplified receptive field. Cells are represented by nine small squares. The cell at the center adds the full value it receives; cells at the border subtract one-eighth of the value received by each of them. At the right illustration, you can see the receptive field applied over a corner of a frame. The cell at the center receives a value of 5; cells at the borders receive values ranging from 4 to 6. The value transmitted by the central cell is $5 - (4 + 4 + 4 + 4 + 4 + 5 + 5 + 6) \div 8 = 0.5$. As this is a positive value, it tells the brain that the point should be perceived lighter. This effect, working over all the corners of all the frames, produces the luminous rays.

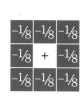

Perhaps you may have noticed in the last illustration that the luminous rays disappear, with only a lighter dot remaining at the frame corners. The reason for this is that the receptive fields in your eyes are small, so the illusion can only be perceived when the figure projects a small image on the retina. That is the reason why you cannot see the luminous rays under a magnifier and also the reason why they will appear again if you move the book away from your eyes.

Interrupted Line

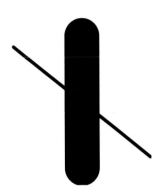

Ask a friend if the right part of the diagonal line above is a continuation of the left part. He or she will probably answer no: the right part seems to be slightly lower. However, both parts do belong to the same straight line. The curious thing is that if instead of a plane figure, we consider the illustration as an object with depth, the continuous line becomes evident. The illustration below is similar to the above but for the white circle. If you look at it using the stereograms technique (see pages 85–88), you'll see a pipe in two versions: in one version the diagonal line passes in front of the pipe; in the other, the diagonal line passes behind. In both, the illusion is gone and the diagonal line is clearly continuous. In addition, when the diagonal line is seen at the front, you can even perceive a ghost figure joining the left and right parts.

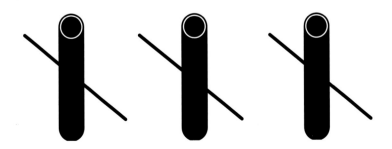

Burn Those Photos!

A quail's feathers match the color of the earth and grass. A jaguar's spots match the play of light and shadow of the Sun passing though the foliage. A chameleon copies the colors of the bough on which it stands. All these animals hide themselves by camouflaging their bodies (the figure) with their surroundings (the ground). These animals do this as a way to hide from predators or prey (so that they are not detected by them). Here, we will use a technique known as "burned photograph" to camouflage figures. Let's look at an example.

The first step is to select an illustration. In our example, we chose the photo of a flamingo.

The next step is to produce a gray-tone version of the image. This can be done with a photo processing program.

Then change the photograph's brightness and contrast so all the middle grays are removed and the result is an image with only two colors:

black and white. Do not do this automatically with the software program. Experiment to find which areas should go white and which should go black. With a little practice, you will get it right.

Notice how you can still recognize the flamingo. This is because you saw the original image before it was processed. If a friend looks at this last image, he or she may be unable to see what it is.

Below are a couple of puzzles. Can you recognize the subjects in the two images? If you can't, go to the answers. With this type of illusion, once you have identified the subject, you will recognize it immediately the next time you see it. It is as if your recognition has changed the image's composition, rearranging its parts in a way that gives it a new meaning.

Answer on page 122.

Changing Images

When using the technique to see stereograms, we have so far looked at two images that were similar or complementary. What happens if both pictures are different—that is, if each eye looks at an image that, in a sense, conflicts with the other?

The two circles below are intended to be seen each with an eye, as you've done in the Third Pole chapter (see page 66), so the brain can merge them into a single image. Notice that each circle is divided into opposite halves: curved red circles against straight green lines. When the brain merges the two circles, the perception is unclear. Sometimes you see a combination of curves and straight lines only to be replaced a moment later by a different scheme. Are your eyes fighting each other to tell your brain what is to be perceived? Nobody is quite sure how it works. Notice how often you can see a complete bull's-eye or a circle filled with horizontal lines.

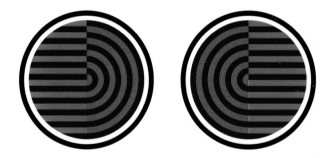

The next illusion shows how the perceived images are replaced. Merge the two circles and notice how the spheres replace the circles, starting from a small area and expanding from there.

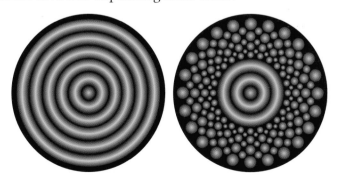

The Making of Mist

In computer vision science, an image is analyzed, separated into individual objects, and then recognized.

One of the main methods used in computer vision is joint analysis. Three different types of joints have been circled in the illustration

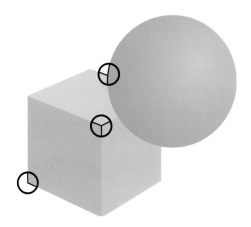

above. The one where two different borders overlap (the borders of the sphere and top of the cube) is called a T-joint, because it looks like a letter T (here, the T is rotated). The joint where a border changes direction (the lower left corner of the cube) is called an L-joint, while the joint where three edges meet is called a Y-joint. These aren't the only joint types. There are, for example, X-joints and even Greek-letter joints: Ψ. Some joints indicate the contour of objects, others indicate interior edges, and some others indicate color differences—be it because the object is painted in different colors, a shadow falls over it, or the object is seen through a semitransparent material, like a tinted glass. One of the greatest challenges of joint analysis is to determine whether a joint represents an object border or a change in color.

X-joints, for example, often represent color changes. Some scientists think our brain, when presented with an X-joint, automatically deduces a change in color. To see how, we will make mist.

We already encountered this when dealing with ghost figures. In the illusion below, the circles are incomplete, so we perceive two diamonds hiding parts of them.

We also encountered the second step: coloring the missing parts of the circles brings on the appearance of ghost diamonds.

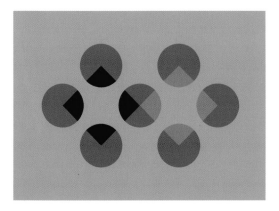

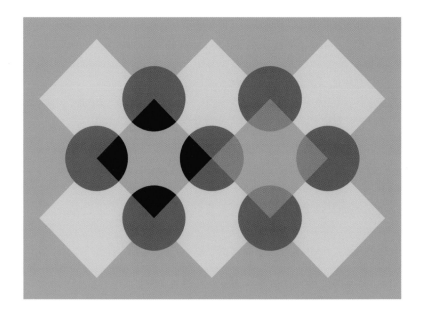

In the last step, we paint light color patches around the ghost diamonds, making sure to leave the circles untouched. In doing this, something weird happens. The ghost diamond at the left changed almost imperceptibly; it is somewhat better defined and the color is probably perceived in a slightly different relation to the background. But the ghost diamond at the right is completely transformed—not only is the color different but the whole square looks milky, as if seen through mist. The effect is so strong that you might like to check if the background is still the same hue as that of the ghost diamonds. Take a piece of paper, cut out three holes matching the background and the diamonds and place it over the illustration.

Enter X-joints here. When we painted the light color patches, we introduced X-joints at the borders of the ghost figures. One of these joints (the one corresponding to a border of the left ghost diamond) is shown in the following page. The X-joint divides the area inside the circle into four fields, every one a different hue. According to scientists, the analysis of the differences among these hues tells our brain how to decode the scene.

The X has two strokes. If the hues at one side of a stroke are always darker than corresponding hues at the other side of the stroke, the perception assumes that there is a shadow or filter on the latter's side.

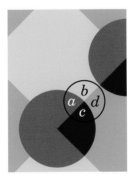

That's the case with the ghost diamond at the left. Considering one of the strokes, regions a and c (that are on the same side) are respectively darker than b and d (that are on the other side of the stroke). That is, a is darker than b and c is darker than d. At the same time, considering the other stroke, c is darker than a and d is darker than b. If you go back to the Tiles and Chessboard chapter (see page 50), you'll see that only the second illustration has this type of X-joint. That is the reason why we saw it as having a shadow cast on it.

The X-joint on the borders of the misted diamond has a different color scheme. Although a and c (which are on the same side of an X stroke) are respectively darker than b and d, along the other stroke,

a is darker than *c* but *b* is lighter than *d*. This particular scheme signals the presence of a mist. Where? Consider the stroke where hues on one side are respectively darker than hues on the other side—in the above illustration, the stroke that divides *a-c* from *b-d*. Mist is always covering the two zones with lesser contrast. As the contrast between *a* and *b* is greater than between *c* and *d*, the mist lies over the latter two regions.

Now, what if along the two X strokes, a color is darker than its correspondent, but the other is lighter? We will see no shadow, filter, or mist—just a change in colors, which is the case with the first and third illustrations in the Tiles and Chessboard chapter.

All of this can be summarized in the following diagram (the symbol > means darker than):

Shadow or filter   *Mist*   *Color*

By rotating and/or reflecting the whole diagram (or an individual stroke within a diagram), you'll get all the possible X-joints.

A final note: all this looks great, but in order to have a joint, you need sharp borders. Have you ever seen a mist with sharp borders? Of course not, mist borders are always diffused.

Illusions Gallery

This last chapter contains a gallery of different optical illusions. Near each illusion are instructions.

LEFT: *If you stare at the woman's face long enough, she will open her eyes and look back at you (Postcard, 1910).*

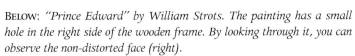

BELOW: *"Prince Edward" by William Strots. The painting has a small hole in the right side of the wooden frame. By looking through it, you can observe the non-distorted face (right).*

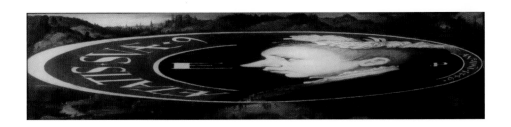

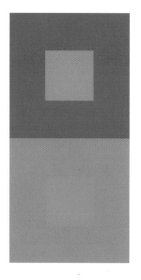  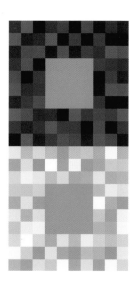

ABOVE: *The central squares are all the same color. But if you alter the hues of the background squares (top left), then the top central square looks slightly lighter than the bottom central square. If the contrast between the backgrounds increases (top center), so does the illusion. If the backgrounds have an average contrast similar to the previous but are made of tiles (top right), the illusion increases even more.*

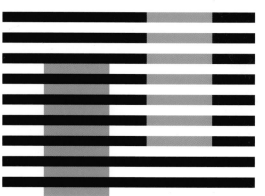

LEFT: *The orange squares set on diagonals (top) and the orange bands (bottom) are all the same color. Notice that in these illusions, as opposed to what happened in the top illusion of central squares, the colors mainly surrounded by a lighter background are seen as lighter.*

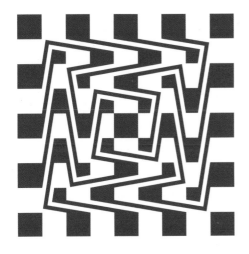

LEFT AND BELOW: *The cords at the left form squares; those below form concentric circles.*

ABOVE AND RIGHT: *Although both figures are made only of squares and straight lines, the upper one seems to bulge at the center while the right one seems to have curved horizontal bands.*

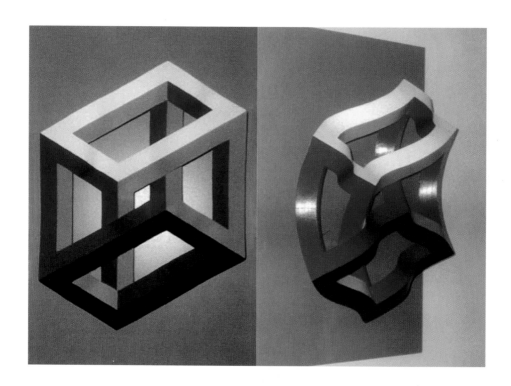

ABOVE AND RIGHT: *"Real Virtuality" by Mathieu Hamaekers. Contrary to virtual reality created by computers, the artist created a real object that looks nonexistent. Seen from the front, it's an impossible figure; seen from another point of view, the seemingly straight bars are discovered to be twisted.*

RIGHT: *"Yellow Stairs" by Alvaho. Both are impossible: the stairs at the right cannot be constructed like that; the ladder at the left cannot be placed like that.*

LEFT: *Although the left square looks darker, it is the same color as the right one. Both are colored in a gradient of blue that darkens toward the right border.*

RIGHT: *The red dots seen at the white corners are an illusion produced by the contrast enhancing system in the retina cells.*

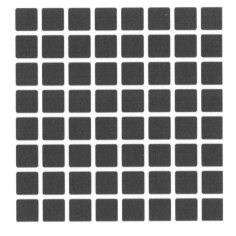

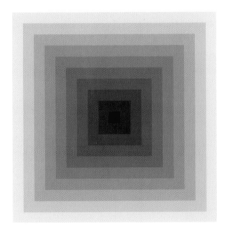

LEFT: *The dark rays transecting the corners are an illusion. They are also produced by the same contrast enhancing system.*

RIGHT: *Bright spots appear at the area where the lines converge.*

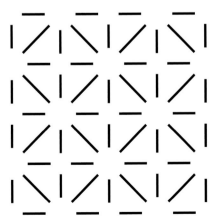

109

ABOVE: *"The Incredible Upside-Downs of Little Lady Lovekins and Old Man Muffaroo," a comic strip by Gustave Verbeek. When seen upside down, the bird's beak is transformed into a boat, the head into a fish, the body into an island, the legs into trees, and the birds on the horizon into waves.*

LEFT: *"Summer" by Giuseppe Arcimboldo. The man's portrait is totally made from fruit, vegetables, and grain stalks.*

LEFT: *Although per-ceived slanted, the lines in the two circles are perfectly horizontal.*

RIGHT: *The black circles create a three-dimensional ghost figure: a pyramid.*

BELOW: *The circles distort the diamond (left). The diamonds distort the circle (right).*

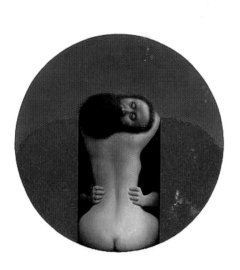

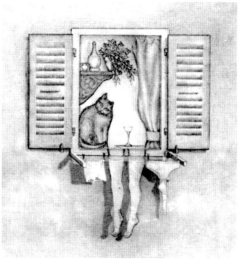

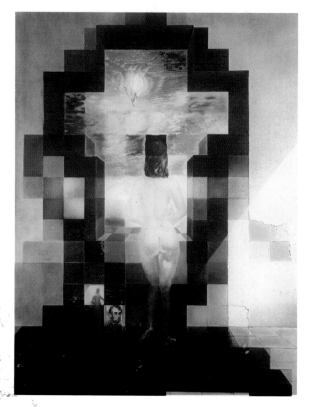

TOP LEFT: *"Nuestro Amor (Our Love)" by Alfredo Castañeda. This is similar to the illusions in the Only One Head chapter. Can you see the face of a man and the head of a woman, or only the face of a man and his beard?*

TOP RIGHT: *"The Window" by Sandro del Prete. The picture is just of a pair of stockings, a cat, a glass, a curtain, a shelf, and a plant. The woman is the product of your imagination.*

LEFT: *"Lincoln" by Salvador Dalí. Up close, you see the back of a woman. From afar (or with half closed eyes), Lincoln's portrait.*

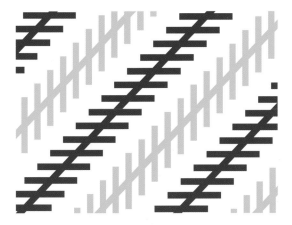

LEFT: *All the diagonal lines are parallel.*

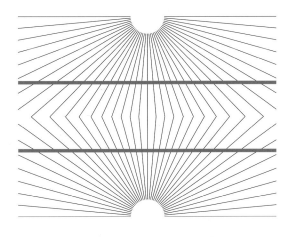

ABOVE: *The horizontal lines are straight but are perceived as curving inward.*

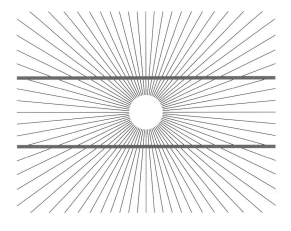

LEFT: *The horizontal lines are straight but are perceived as curving outward.*

RIGHT: *A double portrait. Depending on how you see it, this illusion shows a young lady with her head turned away or the profile of an old lady.*

ABOVE: *Turn the policeman's head upside down to find an angry headmaster.*

BELOW: *Several animals and hunters can be found hiding in the bushes.*

LEFT: *Depending on how you see it, this illusion shows either a yellow wine glass in front of a blue tray or a fat blue worm wrapped around a yellow can.*

RIGHT: *Move the book toward and away from you. Halos will appear and disappear from around the center.*

BELOW: *Two illusions occur here: concentric circles appear around the center and white dots appear where black lines intersect.*

ABOVE RIGHT: *From afar, you can see a woman's face (copied from "The Birth of Venus" by Sandro Botticelli; above left). If you look closer, you will see that the face is made of small tiles, each one a photo of a flower. This technique is known as photomosaic.*

RIGHT: *Enlarged detail of the photomosaic. Can you tell which feature this is? Hint: Look at it from 6 feet (1.8 m) away.*

RIGHT: *Schroeder stairs, a reversible figure, can be perceived as seen from above (the dark zone at the bottom right is the nearest plane), or from below (the dark zone at the top left is the nearest plane).*

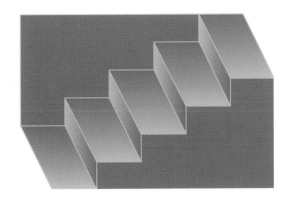

LEFT: *Reversible cubes. The perception alternates between six cubes seen from above and ten cubes seen from below.*

RIGHT: *An impossible polyhedron made from impossible staircases.*

Answers

Turn the Lights Off!

As we have seen, eliminating the blue lines will not get rid of the glow. But if the black lines are removed, the illusion disappears. Another curious way of turning the lights off is to draw little blue strokes intersecting at the point where the black and blue lines meet.

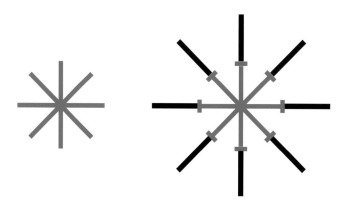

On the other hand, if the blue lines are slightly separated from the black lines (by placing thin strips of paper over their meeting points), the glow disappears but the gap between the lines suddenly forms a halo.

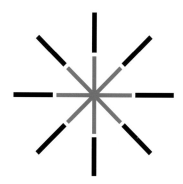

The Size of Heavenly Bodies

The photo shows the Moon (or the Sun; both are seen as the same size in the sky) as it really is. Don't worry if you drew yours larger; all artists do. In fact, we all experience the same visual illusion. If you take a photograph with 35 mm film and a normal camera lens (50 mm focal length) and enlarge it to 4 × 6 inches (10 × 15 cm), the Moon's (or Sun's) diameter will be a hundredth of the diagonal, that is, a trifle smaller than one eighth of an inch. That is exactly the same proportion the Moon has in this photo.

Only One Head

The solution uses the same technique as the Japanese stamp and the Persian dish: each horse head is composed of two bodies, one galloping and the other resting. The figures of the jockeys complete the galloping horses.

Foreground and Background

Where the goblet meets the background shows two profiles. To see them, turn the page upside down. The two faces can be seen more easily over a black background.

Rearranging the parts as shown below, you'll create a galloping white horse over the black background made by the donkey.

The Mountains of the Moon

Turn the illustration 90° clockwise. The raised spheres will form the number 15.

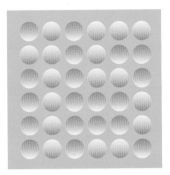

The circles in the puzzle are illuminated from the side and look completely flat. By turning the illustration, the light falls from above and creates an illusion of raised and depressed circles. Now a pattern is formed whereby we can group those that are similar.

Lettering

The order from taller to shorter is star, circle, triangle, and square. Below you can see the figures redrawn all exactly the same height. Now the star looks shorter and the square looks taller.

Burn Those Photos!

The first image shows a leopard; the second image shows the head and part of a cow's body.

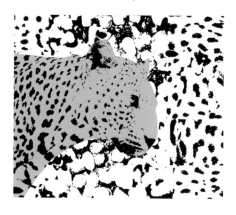 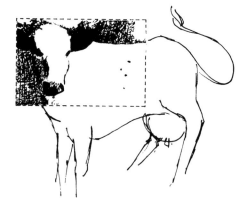

Gravity Lens

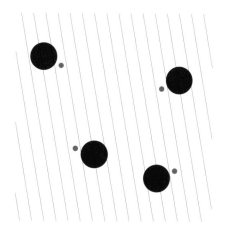

To make the illusion reappear, you must extend the two lines in the puzzle and draw new lines parallel to them. Now the lines are no longer perceived as sides of the parallelogram but as the illustration background.

Extra Columns

The color of one of the columns' sides is actually a uniform shade. It looks darker toward the top than bottom, but if you cover the neighboring sides, you will see that it is actually an even tone. This is also a simultaneous contrast illusion, similar to those in the Shady Comparisons chapter, and is caused by the gradual tone color of the neighboring sides.

Pushing Dots

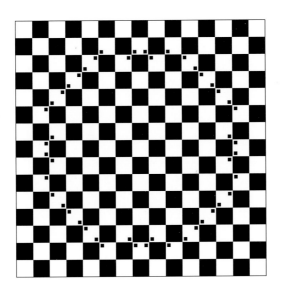

Hide and Seek

The following animals are hidden in the foliage. At the top left is the head of an elephant. Immediately at its right is the dark-colored head of a camel. Below the elephant's trunk is a pig. Somewhat below the pig and at its right is a rabbit. Below this rabbit is a second rabbit. To the right of the first rabbit is an eagle head that is upside down. Below the eagle head is a cat head rotated 90°. At the top right, partially hidden by the tree trunks, is a second, larger elephant head. In the trunk of the nearest tree is an anteater head; its legs are at the right side of the trunk. In the space between two trees is a baboon head that is upside down. At the bottom right is a boar head that is also upside down. And there may be even more animals…

Shady Comparisons

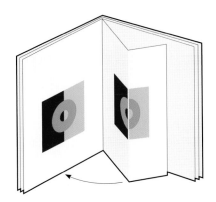

Fold the page as shown, making sure that the white line dividing the ring goes to the inner part of the fold. The figure below will appear when you place the folded page over the previous page. Now the right part of the ring looks much darker than the left part. In a way, it seems as if the darker hue of the navy background at the left continues through the right part of the ring while the lighter hue of the periwinkle background at the right continues through the left part.

References and Credits

Page 6 top: Based on Roger Shepard. Page 8 bottom: Drawing by F. Hausman (Zeller Collection). Page 9 top: ©1996, G. Sarcone (from *Dazzling Optical Illusions*, Sterling Publishing Co.), www.archimedes-lab.org. Pages 14–16: Adapted from V. Ramachandran. Page 17: Based on Whitaker-McGraw. Page 18: Based on D. Purves. Page 29: ©2003, Scott Kim, www.scottkim.com. Page 31: Adapted from E. Adelson. Page 32: Adapted from Koffka. Page 34: Adapted from A. Kitaoka. Page 36: Adapted from E.B. Titchener. Page 38: *"Le Clown Songeur"* by A. Martins de Barros, Paris, France, www.martinsdebarros.com. Page 39: "Shakespeare" by István Orosz. Page 40–42: Based on G. Kanizsa. Pages 43–44: Based on H. Wallach. Page 45: Based on P.U. Tse. Page 47: "Animals in the Wood" ©Anno Mitsumasa. Page 48: Adapted from Muller-Lyer. Page 49: Adapted from Ponzo. Page 50: Adapted from A. Kitaoka. Pages 52 & 53 top: "Tarrant County Civil Courthouse Annex" by Richard Haas, www.richardhaas.com; photos by R. Haas. Page 53 bottom: ©Portmeirion Ltd., www.virtualportmeirion.com. Page 54: Based on D.M. MacKay. Pages 64 & 85: Idea & photo ©2003, Bruno Ernst. Page 65: "Unity" by Mathieu Hamaekers, located at Venlose Steenweg (center of Ophoven), 3640 Kinrooi, Ophoven, Vilaanderen, Belgium. Page 66: Based on C.L. Franklin. Page 66: Based on E. Mach. Page 69: "West Side Story" by István Orosz. Page 70: Based on A. Kitaoka, www.ritsumei.ac.jp/~kitaoka/index-e.html. Page 73: Adapted from S. Naito. Pages 76–77: Photos ©2003, Paul B. Arnold, Oberlin College, Ohio, U.S.A. Page 78 top: Photo ©Philip Greenspun, http://philip.greenspun.com. Page 78 bottom: ©Exploratorium, www.exploratorium.edu. Pages 82 & 83 top: Adapted from J.M. Kennedy. Page 88 top: Based on B. Julesz. Page 88 bottom: Based on Ch. Tyler. Page 89: Based on W. James. Page 90: Based on I. Kojo. Page 91: Adapted from E. Mach. Page 95: Based on Poggendorff. Page 98 bottom: Presented by Dallenbach. Page 99 top: Adapted from E. Díaz Caneja. Page 99 bottom: Based on H.R. Wilson, R. Blake, and S.H. Lee. Pages 101–104: Based on E. Adelson. Page 106 top: Adapted from A. Gilchrist. Page 106 bottom: Adapted from Münker-White. Page 107 bottom: Based on A. Kitaoka. Page 108 top: "Real Virtuality" by Mathieu Hamaekers, located at Venlose Steenweg 81, 3640 Kinrooi, Ophoven, Vilaanderen, Belgium. Page 108 bottom: "Yellow Stairs" by Alvaho (Fred van Houten), www.digitalvaho.myweb.nl. Page 109 top: Adapted from Craik-O'Brien-Cornsweet. Page 109 right: Adapted from Hermann. Page 109 bottom: Based on A.S. Fraser. Page 111 top: Adapted from J.P. Frisby. Page 111 bottom: Adapted from W.O. Orbison. Page 112 top left: *Nuestro Amor* by A. Castañeda. Page 112 top right: "The Window" ©Sandro Del-Prete, www.illusoria.com. Page 113 top: Adapted from F. Zöllner. Page 113 middle & bottom: Adapted from E. Hering. Page 114 top left: Drawing by Whistler. Page 114 top right: Drawing by W.E.Hill. Page 114 middle: Adapted from P.U. Tse. Page 115 top: Adapted from D.M. MacKay. Page 115 bottom: Adapted from N. Wade. Page 117 top: Based on H. Schroeder. Page 117 middle: Based on Necker. Page 118 top right: Adapted from D.D. Hoffman. Page 125 bottom: Adapted from E. Adelson.

Index